Out of Silence

Out of Silence

Carroll Blair

Aveon Publishing Company

Copyright © 2002, 2011, new edition
2025 by Carroll Blair

All rights reserved. No part of this book may be reproduced, or transmitted in any form or by any means, electronic or mechanical, including photocopy, recording, or by any information storage and retrieval system without prior permission of the publisher.

ISBN: 978-1-936430-42-0

Library of Congress Control Number
2011907288

Aveon Publishing Co.
P.O. Box 380739
Cambridge, MA 02238-0739 USA

Also by Carroll Blair

Grains of Thought
Facing the Circle
Reel to Real
Shifting Tides
Reaches
Quarter Notes
By Rays of Light
Into the Inner Life
Gnosis of the Heart
Soul Reflections
Beneath and Beyond the Surface
Of Courage and Commitment
For Today and Tomorrow
In Meditation
Sightings Along the Journey
Through Desert's Fire
Offerings to Pilgrims
Human Natures
(Of Animal and Spiritual)
Atoms from the Suns of Solitude
Colors of Devotion
Voicings
Through the Shadows
As the World Winds Flow

There is music in silence . . . do you hear it
. . . . do you *feel* it . . . .

I

Every day the world is waiting to be discovered.

The Present — The Now . . . this, the eternal moment.

Existence, though constantly changing, is ever complete.

The visible is forever guided by the invisible.

Everything besides being what it is, is a pathway,
an invitation to something else.

What one gets used to one does not see.

Something may begin, yet have no beginning;
something may end, yet have no ending.

It is thought and perception that make the concept of reality
a living entity.

Where the world cannot penetrate . . . that is the place
within oneself that has the power to penetrate the world.

Silence is to thought what space is to matter.

All that happens is seeded in a time before it happens.

There is always a broader lesson to learn from the lesson being learned.

The smallest particle holds within it a universe as mysterious and powerful to the probing mind as the universe itself.

It is the subtle difference that makes all the difference.

Something may be profound in its simplicity, but not simple in its profundity.

Seeing clearly is always seeing with more than just one's eyes.

Wisdom is for all the senses.

Each day whispers to man, "What have you learned from my ancestors . . . will you now learn something from me?"

One cannot perceive the outer world in all its manifestations more deeply than the depths to which one has probed within.

Wisdom comes of its own accord. One cannot find it by searching for it, *but it will not come unless one searches for it.*

Knowledge can be stated in a moment yet take a lifetime to comprehend.

The wise listen closely to the unspoken.

The greater the profundity the more silent, the more calm, the more still.

There is no discovery without losing sight of the familiar.

To get behind the surface of things you must leave yourself behind — (i.e., your "I" behind).

Every breath is a life in itself.

There are times when thought has nothing to do with thinking.

The physical too can be a manifest of the spiritual.

Man has but one life, but he lives many lives . . .

The world was here before you arrived and will be here after you've departed, but for you it wasn't before you, and will not be after you.

In silence every spirit is free.

The quiet mind hears everything.

The greater one's depth the higher degree of consciousness.

There is no ending to the journey of enlightenment.

Every moment of creative bliss contains a spark of the infinite.

As there are creative minds so are there creative hearts.

Emotions are felt most intensely when they and their opposites come closest to being one.

Of all passions the quiet passion is pregnant with the strongest power.

They know something of the impossible who achieve the most distant of possibles.

The value of temporal achievement is measured in grains; the value of immortal achievement, in suns.

Those who reach the summit of the mountain are more conscious of the sky above them than they are the valley below.

Who cannot dream with clarity of vision cannot live with clarity of vision.

The most powerful spiritual lights give one illumination without blinding one from the path that he himself must follow.

No one who has lived with courage dies with fear.

The greatest strength is never without the presence of beauty and grace.

It is death that makes life sacred; it is life that makes death profound.

Sometimes a question is the answer to another question.

Between darkness and light there is more darkness and light.

Every man must error his own way to Truth; each in his own time and in his own fashion.

Man is a possibility . . . only a possibility . . .

To discover your power is to discover your life.

What winds the sails of one ties an anchor to another.

What one does not love one cannot overcome.

He who loves so long as he is loved does not love.

The price of a spiritual lightning is a willingness to sometimes be shattered by the lightning.

There are more blessings to be had from life than anyone has yet to experience.

The nature of the human mind is such that its power to create will always be greater than its power to understand.

What is for all time is for no time (that is to say, is beyond time).

Inspiration is the soul stirring the mind with a kiss.

Nothing substantial can be created without knowledge, but one must *turn one's back on knowledge* while in the process of creating.

Where progression ends, refinement begins.

It is impossible to master anything without also being its servant.

All that's been done had to be done in order to do what is to be done next.

What is *not* is as important as what *is* in regard to maintaining the balance of existence.

If not for something inside you that knew what you were going to do long before you did it, you could never do it.

Everything is interdependent, and life could not exist without this interdependence, but the synthesis of all things would be the death of all things.

There are similarities more irreconcilable than opposites.

If all were easy nothing would please.

Where there is an absence of noble purpose no happiness is possible beyond the ephemeral.

A journey of ten thousand steps is a journey of ten thousand different steps taken by the same pair of feet.

The closer one gets to the mountain the less it looks like a mountain.

There is everywhere and in every thing in this life, instruction.

It is not enough to be smart enough to learn from one's experiences; one must also be brave enough.

Many want to learn, or say they want to learn, but never prepare themselves to receive the lesson.

There is not always a silver lining to a cloud. Sometimes it is gold, but one cannot see it, because his eyes are looking for silver and can't see the gold.

Every soul has its garden, and in this garden there is soil and seed. The soil is talent, the seed, creativity. (A garden that many never discover.)

Long spiritual journeys cannot be taken by the shortsighted or weak of heart.

As iron cannot be forged without hammer and heat, so spiritual strength cannot be forged into beauty and utility without passion and pain.

To always be striving for pleasures and the avoidance of pain at all costs is to strive for banality and away from enlightenment.

The most luminous spirits are they that do not shy away from the offering of their sufferings.

No candle burns for the sake of itself.

What one gives to life draws one closer to life.

One is enslaved by that which one is unable to share.

All good things of the soul are arrived at, not coming from out of the blue (or the dark).

Something may be fragile, though noble, yet nothing can be weak, though noble.

The flower not only needs its days of sun, but also its days of rain.

The most instructive lessons of life are without words.

Inches above the rumblings of an earthquake the air remains calm, tranquil, undisturbed . . .

The temporal is full of noise; the eternal, filled with silence.

Falsehood shouted from the rooftop has not the power of a whispered truth.

Illusion can take one far out into the ocean of one's journey, but it will never guide one to land.

It is possible to create in the dark only when one has been schooled in the light.

Creativity . . . if not the highest intelligence, then higher than intelligence.

Everything is a prolusion to what comes next.

The most profound changes of mind and spirit are the most subtle.

The invisible is needed as much as the visible to ascend to higher levels of being. (Without the space between the steps of the stairs, there would not be stairs.)

How to live becomes an easier question to answer when one's *why* to live has been found.

Not every moment of a life is remarkable, but every one necessary to get to the moments that are.

Sometimes the loss of something valuable leads to the gain of something even more valuable.

The most noble rising, and ultimately the most beautiful is the rising from the ash.

In the spiritual realm all negatives can be transformed into positives, or placed in the service of the positive.

It is challenge that sets one on one's way to truth.

What it costs someone to learn something can never be known by another.

It requires wisdom to recognize folly, but also to recognize wisdom.

The courage to leave the past, live the present and face the future is all one.

The wise always look beyond what is before them, but also *see* what is before them.

As the properties of physical light are the same in all ages, so the properties of spiritual light are the same in all ages.

There is no movement in spiritual growth where the heart cannot be moved.

The further one needs to travel to attain enlightenment, the less awareness one has of the distance.

All life generates from the inside out, yet some strive and many look for change to come from the outside.

The world pains more than it has to when man endures less than he needs to.

One must say no many times before one is able to utter the eternal *yes*.

There is the will to live, and the will to *life*.

In the highest spheres of consciousness blame does not exist.

Because something is one thing or another doesn't mean that it can't also be something else, or other things . . . (even many things).

He dreams a perpetual dream who believes that everything he sees is exactly as he sees it.

Though it may seem incomplete to the human eye nothing perishes before completing its business on the stage of Life.

Forever *for you* is only as long as the time that you are.

The time of pregnancy of what is born in a moment of your life is all the moments of your life that have gone before it.

One builds everything on what one already has.

To draw closer to life is to move deeper into oneself.

One's path is also one's guide.

The personal questions of a life can never be answered by another.

There is something higher, more distinguished, more *beneficial* than believing in oneself, and that is *to be free of the need* to believe in oneself.

Rare is the one who is able to love beyond the dictates of one's needs.

To be loved is not as important as to be worthy of being loved.

It requires a strong sense of self-awareness to reach the noble state of selflessness.

One cannot know anything beyond the superficial without knowing oneself beyond the superficial.

No riches of the world can fill the void of a barren inner life.

To possess is often to destroy.

How many victories bear the look of defeat, and defeats, the look of victory.

One may live many moments of life, even every moment of life, with Illusion, but no moment can be *lived* without Truth.

There is great strength in the willingness to doubt.

All are unique in their emotions; few are unique in their thoughts.

It is easier to find meanings in the world than it is to find meaning.

Metaphysics paws the sacred ground where Reason stands watch.

The long ago lies mummified awaiting the clarity of tomorrow.

Insight . . . the moment of understanding that grants yet one more piece to the puzzle of existence, one more glimpse into its mystery.

Beneath the tree of knowledge there is shade.

No understanding of opposites can exist without an understanding of both opposites.

At the foundation of comprehension is reflection and interpretation.

The most subtle observations make for the most powerful impressions.

The sense of awe is the sense of immensity.

To be able to contemplate what the universe is made of, how it works and how it came to be is as fascinating as the universe itself.

The imagination doesn't take one only to places of fantasy, but also to places of undiscovered realities.

There is still new in much of the old that has yet to be discovered.

Inside every kernel of thought there's an epic waiting to unfold.

Ideas are nurtured in the heart as much as they are in the mind.

The mind and heart are sun and rain to each other, and the soul a rainbow to both.

To feel the sacredness of life with every atom of one's being, if only once, and if only for a brief moment, is a most rare and wondrous gift.

There are things higher than what is often referred to as "success."

The perfect offering is prepared without audience and delivered without fanfare.

One cannot use that which one loves; one can only serve what one loves.

Beauty . . . the daughter of Subtlety and Grace.

Genius comes and goes like the wind, but like the wind, is always present *somewhere*.

The greater the idea the more mysterious its source and manner of coming.

The great exchange: An "I" (ego) for an "eye" (spiritual).

To detach oneself from the *self* of oneself . . . here lies the key to the beginnings of true self-awareness.

One acquires a better view of an entire room by standing in a corner than by standing at its center.

Experience is a classroom only to the wise.

One never stumbles into the Temple of Wisdom by chance nor gains entrance through its doors by sleeping on its steps.

It is the easiest path that leads to nowhere.

Every depth has its surface, but not every surface has its depth.

The most tragic figure of all is he who has never known tragedy.

Of Life: the magic is in the struggle, the miracle is in the result.

It is the ventures in human endeavor that have the greatest potential for danger that humankind can least do without.

Until engaging the work of inner growth the truth of one's measure cannot be known.

What one is able to perceive has the profoundest influence on what one is able to be, spiritually speaking.

It takes a greater courage to face one's strength than it does to face one's weakness.

To see things differently is (more often than not) to see things more clearly.

Where the largest gatherings are to be found . . . these are the points that are furthest away from truth.

Illusion is a warm blanket that turns cold upon its subject's awakening.

In the life of the average spirit it is the eternal that is ignored and the ephemeral that is embraced.

In the world of creativity the stream that barely trickles is superior to the large body of stagnant water.

To create in the aim of the good is to love.

No one can truly own anything but the riches of mind, heart and spirit that are one's own.

The richer one's inner world the less one needs from the outer world, yet the more one may contribute to it.

Love is the force that keeps one joined to one's duty with loyalty and dedication.

Spiritually speaking the most difficult tasks bring forth the finest fruit.

It is in the spiritual dimension of humankind where a meaning for its existence and unity of purpose may be achieved.

The life of every human is a call to speak his or her soul.

A baby learns to cry before it learns to laugh, but also to sing before it learns to talk, and dance before it learns to walk.

Every day a stroke is added to the portrait of one's life.

As long as you breathe, Life has made a commitment to you. Have you made a commitment to Life?

II

Your life is a product of creation. Is it not, therefore, meant to be a vessel of creation?

The mind . . . a microcosm of the universe; the universe . . . a macrocosm of the mind.

In a second a thought can flash across the mind that will live for centuries, yet it has taken billions of years to come into being.

The highest things are beyond the realm of thought, but nothing in man is greater than his ability to conceive and comprehend thought.

Opinion gives people a say in the world, thought gives them a place.

The mind has wisdoms of its own and for its own that one can never know.

As space allows for matter to be, so that which doesn't exist or never happens allows what does to be.

The influences of life are so subtle and far-reaching that not one atom of existence would be the same if one atom were missing.

Knowledge is always a step or more behind the imagination.

Regarding the physical everyone is made from the same material; not so, the spiritual.

The most noble paths in life are not those that become easier with time, but harder.

The spirit beckons to go forward, to ignore much, to leave much behind, with the promise of insight lighting in the distance waiting for those who heed the call . . . (how few heed the call).

The essence of spirituality (or of a spiritual life) is selflessness.

Wisdom, Justice, Love, Nobility . . . they do not rule the world, but do their best to serve it.

It takes less evil to poison much in the world than it takes good to heal a little.

While most have their eyes fixed on the clouds overhead, the wise have their eyes on the clouds approaching.

To the truly observant nothing looks the same way twice.

Where you have walked, things will never be the same. Perhaps in the humblest ways, but nevertheless . . . never the same.

You have your whole life to thank or curse for the moment you are experiencing *now*.

What is possible for you to know in precisely the way you know it can never be learned from another *or by another*.

One leaves as much of oneself with a profound experience as one takes with him or her.

Inspiration takes note of what one does while awaiting its coming.

The depth of one's abyss determines the height of bliss that one is capable of experiencing.

Spiritually speaking many live too little because they die too little.

Great things are delicate things.

The highest and rarest of beauty is spiritual beauty.

One comes closest to understanding the nature of Life who understands the nature of suffering.

What rises is not noticed as readily as what falls.

The tree drops the fruit that clings too long.

What is truly felt is truly suffered.

Only nothingness is able to embrace all.

To doubt is to know.

From a billion possibilities, a fraction of realities.

A truth may be told in parts, but Truth can not.

It is Truth and Beauty, not man that is the measure of all things.

Man spends his whole life trying to escape the one thing that can save him and give his life meaning, which is his suffering.

Spiritual struggle is the great pain yet also the great happiness; material struggle the great misery.

The deeper the mind the more clearly it can perceive the immense void that compels one searcher to flee and another to face his nothingness.

One must lose oneself in order to find oneself.

Few end their lives in the same key that it began.

Harmony . . . the reverie of entropy.

Time is eternal virginity.

The goal of evolution is a striving toward infinite beginnings, not a journey to an ultimate end.

It is the highest spirits that feel their lowliness most intensely before the totality of all there is.

Remove the delusion of self-importance from one's life and all delusions vanish.

One who has not purged himself of ego's base manifests is like a chickling that has yet to crack open its shell.

Sometimes the desire to give is the desire to take something away.

Not every increase is a gain.

All life is a sacrifice.

There is truth behind all that is sincere, if only the truth of its sincerity.

No one knows what others have endured or can endure; only what they could not endure.

The world casts suspicion on what has not been created before its eyes.

The passions that inspire the spirit to take flight are not the same as the passions that inspire to sustain it.

Emotion also has its consciousness and subconsciousness.

To go beyond you must first go below.

In life some things go to you, and some things you must go to.

Who seek the full light of spirituality cannot avoid an odyssey through a darkness of equal measure.

There is mystery in all that is profound.

Spiritually speaking some pray to protect themselves from the rain while others pray for the lightning.

One is most vulnerable to fall to one's lowest weakness when nearing the pinnacle of one's greatest strength.

Innocence is such a beautiful and precious thing, something that the world would be left poorer and less beautiful if without, but *to appreciate the beauty and value of innocence, innocence must be lost.*

Sufferings of today are as coals that may one day transform into spiritual diamonds.

To know when you don't know is a powerful piece of knowledge; when you don't understand, a powerful understanding.

For every hundred who are listening, one is hearing; for every thousand who are looking, one is seeing.

More are blind to all but their own vision, deaf to all but their own song than most would suspect.

There are more invisible barriers between human beings than there are visible.

As various sea animals live at different depths of the ocean, so various humans live at different depths of life.

Humble beings even the greatest of humans must be; whether they know it or not, whether they like it or not.

Every force has its limits.

No one profits from all that one knows.

Wisdom can only be a friend to the world; the same cannot be said of knowledge.

The more dependent man becomes on technology the freer he thinks he is.

Some lives are too full to be rich.

To speed things up spiritually speaking one must slow things down literally speaking.

How much one gains by learning to do without.

Wisdom births in quiet places.

Every moment is a wakeup call to life if one stills to listen.

One learns more about life (and more importantly, what it means to be *alive*) by having an intense interest and focus on one thing than a trivial interest in many things.

Some make of their life a mere existence; others make of their existence a passionate life.

One doesn't drown in the depths of human spirit, but in its shallows.

The only thing that is feared more by most than staring into the face of death is staring into the face of truth.

To be afraid of death is to be afraid of nothing, for that is precisely what death is: nothing — (even if there is something beyond the grave).

Individual life dies, but Life never dies.

The river pays no heed to yesterday's flow.

Only the work that one lives for when one lives can live for others when one is no more.

For every death never to be again a life takes its place, never to be again.

Every person is a once-in-a-lifetime, a once-in-an-eternity, but few accomplish anything that is equal to the uniqueness of their existence.

Of life there are no masters; there are only students.

The world is a schoolroom for some, a schoolyard in recess for others.

Everything that exists can be used to express or explain something else.

All knowledge feeds from other knowledge.

Evolution of the heart is a slower progression than evolution of the mind.

In the world of abstraction too it is at the beginning of something where its chances for survival are most vulnerable, its possibilities for growth and development most fragile.

To the extent that it may be discovered, one must ultimately discover the *how* or *wh*y of anything on one's own.

Nothing keeps one in the dark more than certainty.

Not all illusions are made of air; some are made of brick.

It is the challenges of life that challenge one's notions about life.

Among the most elusive entities in all of existence is the present.

Like the future, the past also has its unexpecteds.

The lifetime of a consequence far exceeds the time of the action from which it manifests.

Every day is a yesterday in the making.

An important question for every human being to ask himself or herself is: "Are you more in tune with is, or IS?" . . . i.e., with the temporal or the eternal?

What is the mind for but to transcend the limits of the physical?

Millions of people every day go to any length within their power to survive without a thought of what it is they are surviving for.

One must get beyond oneself to go beyond anything else.

It is they who have cultivated the highest discipline who have known the highest joyfulness.

There are potentially great riches to be had from the profound pain, none from the shallow pleasure.

Among the things most rarely understood by human beings is the gift of tragedy.

Suffering too has its stages of maturity.

The true progress of human life is not a progression of ease and comfort, but the progression of spiritual development.

A powerful moment in a life is when it is ready for something extraordinary that it has never been ready for.

Of spiritual gifts, what one gives generously has not been acquired freely or easily.

Sometimes the roadblocks that are placed in the path of one's life prevent one from journeying to a dead end, creating detours that lead to discoveries never imagined.

If one were to be shown at the beginning of one's life the journey one was to take in all its detail it would not be believed, yet the reflective spirit looking back at the end of life could not imagine the journey to be otherwise.

Through his play man demonstrates much of who he is; through his work he demonstrates all of what he is.

The power to destroy is second only to the power to create.

Purpose is not something that one is born with; it is something that one either creates or doesn't create in the course of a life.

As one must be in order to do, so one must do in order to be.

Like the sun, some of the brightest spirits of humankind rise without applause.

Just as one's eyes are of little value to one when in the darkness, so is one's goodness worth little to one or anyone else when buried in the cellar of one's soul.

Who starts from the point of metaphysics moves toward clarity; who starts from the point of clarity moves toward the metaphysical.

One could look out a window at the same view every day for a hundred years and not see everything there is to see.

It requires the greatest of imaginations to imagine the realities of existence.

Every facet of a life, though all not wonderful, is still all a wonder.

It is possible for something to be fresh for an eternity, but nothing of the temporal can be new beyond a moment.

One comes to know the relations of things as much by their differences as by their similarities.

Nature's genius is even more subtle than the most subtle of minds suspect.

Nothing beneath the sun is known to everyone.

In the acquisition of knowledge not every truth is more helpful than every error.

Everything strives to be what it is from one moment to the next.

Unlike man, never does Nature destroy without creating something in its place.

Eruption either visible or invisible, audible or inaudible is at the core of everything that comes into being.

What is referred to as a contradiction is sometimes a union between opposing concepts or energies that transcends one's ability to understand their harmony.

Paradox is to Thought what counterpoint is to music.

Everything belongs to itself yet is part of everything else.

It is conceivable to not believe in divinity, yet to still believe in the divine.

The best of the mystical is like beautiful mathematical equations that can never be proved or disproved.

There are always x factors in what it is that makes people what they are.

Of life some people are proud just to be able to survive; others despair because they fail to reach the summit.

It is the few who give serious thought to all.

The best teachers are the lifelong students.

Everyday opinions are as plentiful as the earth's stones; thoughts that transcend the temporal, as rare as its gold.

What one fills one's days with as opposed to another makes all the difference.

A human being is weighted down by everything he or she possesses that does not exist within himself or herself.

Higher than seeking happiness in life is creating a self that merits the gift of life.

All lasting gifts to the world and to oneself are born of creativity.

There is a soul of mind, a heart of soul, a mind of heart . . .

The greatest physical strength cannot compete with the slightest strength of the spiritual.

True power is of the lives of those who do not seek or strive for power outside themselves.

What comes *from you* can never be taken from you.

They are the freest who are neither slave nor master.

A prison can be a palace for he who builds his own prison.

Discipline can be without greatness, but greatness cannot be without discipline.

To spend one's life in the pursuit of illusory power outside oneself is to abandon the source of true power within.

As scraps from a beggar's table is the material wealth of the world compared to a single pearl of spiritual treasure.

No one escapes the consequence of neglecting the inner work.

One can fill the moments of one's life only as substantively as the life that one is filled with.

What a difference there is between an experience of enjoyment and that of joy.

Whatever experience one may share with others it is always (in its final measure) an emprise of one.

With every work of art the artist says to the world "This is what I saw — this is what I thought — this is what I felt — make of it what you will, if you will."

When one can no longer be flattered . . . how much this matters for the maturation process of mind and spirit.

Though only the greatest of them succeed, every artist worthy of the name engages in the soul-splitting task of turning his or her spiritual waters into wine.

Only the strongest souls can conceive the greatest art, and only the strongest hearts can bear it.

As great suffering is not for the faint of heart, so is great joy not for the faint of heart.

There is no place for ego in the profound; ego belongs to the shallows.

The more one truly becomes, the less one feels oneself to be.

The better life is the life that is always trying to do better.

Every day many strive to gain some material possession or other, while some strive to rid themselves of some folly or trivial desire.

How many have ventured into the world without having first ventured into the world of thought . . .

The most important knowledge that is acquired with the growing of awareness is the knowledge of how vast is the universe of one's ignorance.

Logic is the stoic guardian of the sound mind.

The benefit that accompanies the knowledge that one doesn't know everything is the opening of oneself to the counsel of everything.

Everyone is familiar with self-concern; not everyone is familiar with self-examination.

People do not begin to truly live as human beings until they realize that their lives are not about "them."

The ignoble of spirit give others their pain; the noble give others the fruits of their sufferings.

What some have discovered while they were lost has helped others to find their way.

Every day gives man another chance to make right today what he failed to do right yesterday.

It is better than wise to keep in mind that Time is infinite, but one's time is not . . . that Life is infinite, but one's life is not.

In the end all must stand on what they are.

The noise of all worldly glories fades to nothing.

Finding one's way to the spiritual can be difficult, but once found it is like a force or current that takes one to where one needs to go (like a forest fraught with difficulty that one needs to journey through to get to a river, ready to take one home).

The wave of one's life can deliver treasure or trifle to the shore of Eternity.

And in the end, what difference does it make where you are in the outside . . . what difference doesn't it make where you are in the inside . . .

Man searches far to find what is closest to him.

To be full is to be empty in the realm of the physical.

The great gain of life is in the practice of letting go.

Reality has more to do with the invisible than it does the visible.

The ability to contemplate the eternal allows one to share, while one lives, in the wonder of the eternal.

The mind's eye, the spirit's eye, the heart's eye . . . all superior to the physical eye.

Because life itself is paradoxical, would not the highest understanding of it also be paradoxical?

Life educates a hundred percent of the time, but man is conscious of its instruction only a small fraction of the time.

It requires more than thought to inspire the belief that one has hit upon an important wisdom or truth; one must also *feel* it.

Thought is as much a prison as any other, but its cells have no locks or chains.

What binds one also frees one from many things.

No more than anyone can be everywhere at all times does anyone belong everywhere.

All have within them the power to create themselves, but few have the courage to do so.

Every soul is virgin soil.

As sunlight sometimes makes the eyes squint with pain, so spiritual light sometimes makes the soul wince with pain.

What are growing pains of the body compared to the growing pains of the spirit . . .

Suffering is not an enemy but a friend, not a hindrance but an aid, not a curse but a blessing to those who open themselves to its counsel.

To get to the peace one must go through the struggle.

It is the lows of life that seed the coming of its highs.

Sometimes the muse brings her gifts in pieces, like a bird building her nest one piece at a time.

The tree that bears fruit does not consume its fruit.

Symbolism can be perceived in everything if one takes the time to look and makes the effort to see.

Nothing is more difficult in art or in life than reaching the heart of Simplicity.

In a painted picture the paint is not the painting.

Great art doesn't promise a good time, only a profound confrontation.

All art speaks directly, though indirect are many of its interpretations.

Between genius and genius there are also eternities.

Death can no more take the great work into its claws than the lion can take the eagle from the sky.

No one can summon the power of genius. One can only serve it when in its presence and be humbled by it.

A quiet place is music to the creative spirit.

The great joy is in accomplishment driven by love.

What one is able to bring to life becomes a part of life.

Courage stands behind all that is noble.

One doesn't have to create some "thing" in order to create *something*.

Some people make the course of their lives beautiful, like a flower opening steadily to the sun.

Rare is the one who lives for as long as he lives.

How can one live each day anew if one hasn't thought new thoughts, felt new feelings, or experienced new experiences?

When starting the journey into the unknown it makes a difference from where one is standing mentally and spiritually.

The courage of the spirit explorer is sometimes tested, like one who hears the sound of a rattler . . . will he flee from its sound, or investigate from where it is coming . . .

There are spirit warriors who are also deserving of the purple heart.

Wounds either deepen the heart or harden it, depending on the wound, depending on the heart.

Life vetoes nothing, cancels nothing, crosses nothing out.

In every moment of your existence you have everything you need to exist, though perhaps not everything you want.

How fortunate one may be to be handed great misfortune, or unfortunate to be handed great fortune . . .

Sometimes one is not elevated in triumph but diminished.

How much greater is the value of understanding than praise.

It is not the best of humankind that preoccupy themselves with being thought of as best.

The generosity of refrainment or self-restraint not born out of fear is rarer than the generosity of giving.

Life excludes no one from the invitation to live less selfishly, to become more kind, more generous, more noble.

One is challenged by life not only to do better, but also to help others to do better.

It is a greater privilege to teach another than it is to be taught by another.

Everything one says and does to others affects what they subsequently say and do for the rest of their days (be it in the subtlest way).

Sometimes the best lesson one imparts to another is a lesson one never knew that he or she gave.

Rarely does the heart and mind learn things in the same tempo or at the same time.

Some of life's puzzles are a matter of filling in the blanks; others are a matter of finding them.

One always gains when looking for something lost providing one's eyes are open to other things in the search besides what has been lost.

What, once having occurred, and added to all that has gone before it, could be thought of as happening any other way than it happened?

Might not *everything* that comes your way be necessary for you to continue on your way . . .

Symbols are portals and pathways to deeper realities than those of everyday "reality."

To the question, "Where have you been?" how many ever answer or think of answering in reference to anything other than the physical?

For every empirical reality there are multiple realities of the mind.

The further one is from silence the further one is from connecting with the sacred.

Silence is the messenger of the eternal.

The world of the temporal is a world of smoke and mirrors.

The fleeting has many temptations, many transient pleasures that are hollow, that keep one from the true mission of life — the building of the spiritual life.

What good is the power in a soul that lies dormant, never set free to grow . . .

To surpass today what you did yesterday you must go deeper than you did yesterday — into yourself.

In the realm of the spiritual one ascends by way of descending.

What doesn't convulse does not convince in the deepest recesses of mind, heart and spirit.

As there are fears of heights, so are there fears of depths.

The feeling of shattering bones can be less painful than that of shattered illusions.

The most despairing moment of a life could also be its greatest, the moment being central to the best that is to come.

Wisdom abandons no one who has the courage to stand by her.

Dogma is to the imagination what poison is to blood.

Everyone's mind is their own inviolable sanctuary that no one has the right to trespass.

One needn't speak of gods to act first and foremost on the principles of spirituality.

As long as one breathes there is duty to perform.

You see the truth when you find the courage to face what is false.

The power to emancipate is far greater than the power to subjugate.

What is done is not so important as what it leads to.

When the heart is in the right place everything else seems to fall into place.

They have no fear of growing old who have built an inner life rich in wisdom and beauty.

Nobility of character begins where self-interest above all else ends.

Love too has its poetry.

Love and happiness also have their achievements — (i.e., profound love, profound happiness).

What is the aim of human life, the aim that once achieved makes possible the realization of all other aims, if not to go forward without fear . . .

As one empties oneself of banality and pettiness one fills oneself with depth.

Many grow up not wanting to learn but learning to want.

It is impossible to need the wrong things; not so, to want them.

With every compromise in the significant matters of your life a piece of yourself is forever lost.

One must feel the thorns before becoming the rose.

If you believe in what you are doing, what does it matter if no one else believes . . . If you don't believe in what you are doing, what would it matter if everyone else believed . . .

Hope is a child searching for its mother, its father, its brothers and sisters, its unborn sons and daughters . . .

Of the highest things that humankind has achieved, the least knowledge of how it achieves will be found.

It is the *ceaselessness* of Life's energy that is most remarkable and awe-inspiring in Life's grand mystery.

All exist in the midst of a miracle every moment of their life (the miracle being Life itself).

A human being is to the universe what an atom is to the sun. Hence one's significance and insignificance.

No creator heretofore has matched the creative power of the forces that brought him or her into being.

God or no God, the spark that ignited Creation was indeed a divine one.

To some, God is the great question; to others, the great answer.

A glimpse at the shadow of Life's whole would be worth more than the knowledge of a billion of its particulars.

It is not for man to see all there is to see.

If not for man's imagination the world to him would be lost.

Life is a panorama of paradox and contradiction infinitely rich in both order and chaos.

All things are connected, but all things do not harmonize.

One comes to learn through life experience that certain combinations of entities equal something else.

Every moment is complete unto itself, yet a series of moments in sequence renders them incomplete.

Gravity restricts one's freedom of movement, but without it there would be zero freedom of movement.

It is the dizzying speed of earth's rotation and journey around the sun that enables one to move slowly through space and time.

Everything that is known to exist is part of a whole that can never be known (and perhaps this whole, part of a greater whole).

Life is a temporary loan of energies that may be transformed into power.

Nature has nothing to do with sense, yet it makes perfect sense.

Without uttering a word Nature can teach you more than any human could ever teach you.

The further man removes himself from the natural world the greater his loss and more costly his gains.

The visible of the natural is metaphor of the spiritual.

Nature brings forth freely, without desire.

Everything that lives is constantly changing, yet the laws that govern these changes never change.

Every particle of life carries within it the secrets of life.

"What is life about?" . . . the question that rarely leaves the mind of the true thinker — the question from which so many others arise.

If there is an answer to life's mystery, this is profound. If there is not an answer, this is also profound.

The spirit of existence is more powerful than existence itself.

That which endures is that which no power in the universe can destroy.

He lives, but does not *live* who preoccupies himself with the fleeting.

It is not for the herd-human that the prophet goes to the desert or the martyr to the flames.

To be a man or a woman is easier than to be a human being.

The saddest loneliness can be known only to those who are never alone.

They give most to the world who are least of the world.

No one can reflect, imagine, create or understand beyond the range of one's spiritual light.

Only when bearing a wisdom that cannot be put into words is one ready to speak true wisdom.

There are golden rules that are only gold plated.

Religion-wise man has always been overfed, but spiritually he is underfed.

Physical labor is sometimes difficult; spiritual labor, always.

The mountain doesn't reshape itself or make itself smaller to accommodate the one who ventures to climb it.

Every challenge is an invitation to growth.

The one who often reflects on how far he has come is not likely to go as far as the one who reflects on how far he needs to go.

They are most courageous who go a step further than all laws of courage say that they may go.

In the heights of the spiritual opposites become closer to being one, except the eternal and the ephemeral (which become more distant and pronounced).

One cannot move on to higher things without taking with him a more highly developed inner being.

Though everything one does is not profound it has a profound effect on what one does next.

In the realm of spirituality adjusting to the altitude and adjusting to the depth is one and the same.

The closer one gets to the eye of life's pain the more it shines with imperial beauty.

Of all the voices expressed in the world suffering is the most haunting, but also the most beautiful.

Higher love leads everywhere into the arms of affirmation.

The way to salvation is not the way to the cross, it *is* the cross.

Life must be *lived* in order to be received.

If life were easy what would its virtue be . . . what could it be?

Hard work always pays off, but not always when one would like it to, or in the manner of payment one would like to receive.

The extraordinary is not achieved by ordinary means.

For the human being, just "being" isn't enough . . . (is never enough).

Man must journey to the farthest reaches of inner possibilities to bring the slightest measure of profundity to external change.

How many things go into the creation of one significant thing.

There is always something indefinable, something that is added to or holds together or unifies the attributes that are necessary for greatness of spirit to flourish.

No fruit is ripe in its infancy.

A dark truth adds more light than a bright illusion to the path that leads to maturity and self-realization.

It is by thinking for oneself that one creates a self that has the capacity to grow.

One can never be what one does not will.

There is the will of the species, and the will of the individual.

What moves one to go in search of one's best is part of one's best.

No one can get to what is inside you but you.

To never engage in the inner journey is to live a life of motion without movement.

The most spiritually evolved want nothing of others but that they want everything of themselves, i.e., to achieve everything that they are capable of achieving through spiritual energy and love.

What is the purpose of human life if not to transcend its animal dimension?

Man is not yet what he needs to be, to be where he needs to be.

Ego – avarice – base ambition . . . acquiring many "things," but blocking the way to the highest things.

Only the priceless has true value.

Profound joy cannot be inspired by the fleeting.

Many among the most hurried give the least thought to where they are going.

The world does what it wills to those whose inner world is asleep.

The moment lives for the one who lives in the moment.

Everything that lives through the centuries, that breathes in the heart of Eternity was conceived in an intense living of a present.

The eternal cannot be anything but true; can the temporal be anything but false . . .

Time has nothing to do with age, or age with time, spiritually speaking.

Only what comes from the soul has the power to touch the soul.

The spiritual power of one is greater than the political power of all.

One could conquer the world and it would not be as great a feat as the mastering of oneself.

The best that could be granted to you in your life could not be granted by any human being, except yourself.

Should not all that one is able to give to life that contributes to its spiritual dimension be given?

Your past has given you your present. What will your present give to the future . . .

Love, wisdom, truth . . . not only to be found, but also to be created.

Life: the unfinished masterpiece.

The last day of Creation has never ended.

Sing your melody, bring forth *your* song. The earth awaits it — the heavens demand it.

"Thy kingdom come, Thy will be done" . . . . only if we build the kingdom ourselves.

ABOUT THE AUTHOR

Carroll Blair is an author of more than twenty books and the recipient of numerous awards. His work has been well endorsed and commendably reviewed. Among his titles cited for distinction are *Through the Shadows*, winner of the Pacific Book Awards, and *Quarter Notes,* winner of the Sharp Writ Book Awards. He is an alumnus of the Boston Conservatory and lives in Massachusetts.

www.ingramcontent.com/pod-product-compliance
Lightning Source LLC
Chambersburg PA
CBHW031401040426
42444CB00005B/382